Marie Curie

DDLEBACK
ATIONAL PUBLISHING

Saddleback's Graphic Biographies

SADDLEBACK
EDUCATIONAL PUBLISHING
www.sdlback.com

ISBN-10: 1-59905-226-1
ISBN-13: 978-1-59905-226-7
eBook: 978-1-60291-589-3

Printed in Malaysia

20 19 18 17 16   6 7 8 9 10

On a May night in 1902, in Paris, Marie and Pierre Curie went to the old shed where Marie had spent many years of hard work. In the darkness, they saw a beautiful light. No one had ever seen it before. It was the glow of radium.

Marie Curie, the discoverer of radium, was the first great woman scientist—and the first person ever to win two Nobel prizes. She gave the world a new branch of science and a new medical treatment.

She began life as Marya Sklodowska in Warsaw, Poland.

My dear children, your mother has just presented you with a new baby sister, Marya!

When will we see her?

Her father, Professor Sklodowski, was a professor of physics. Even as a small child, Marya loved to look at the instruments he used.

You are a funny child! Do you like my physics apparatus?

Physics ap-par-at-us! Yes!

Marya never forgot anything. She did not forget this. Someday she would learn to use it.

Warsaw was in a part of Poland conquered and ruled by Russia. Everyone had to use the Russian language. It was forbidden to study Polish history or literature.

But some patriotic teachers taught it in secret. Marya's was one of them.

Marya, tell us about Stanislas Augustus.

He was elected King of Poland in 1764. He was intelligent and well-educated.

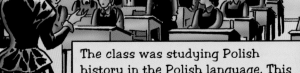

The class was studying Polish history in the Polish language. This was a crime!

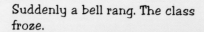
Suddenly a bell rang. The class froze.

The signal! Quick, girls!

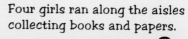
Four girls ran along the aisles collecting books and papers.

They ran with them to another room.

Get out your sewing!

They returned to their seats as the door opened. It was the headmistress with the Russian school inspector.

This is a sewing class. While the girls work, I read them Russian fairy tales!

H'm ... I see.

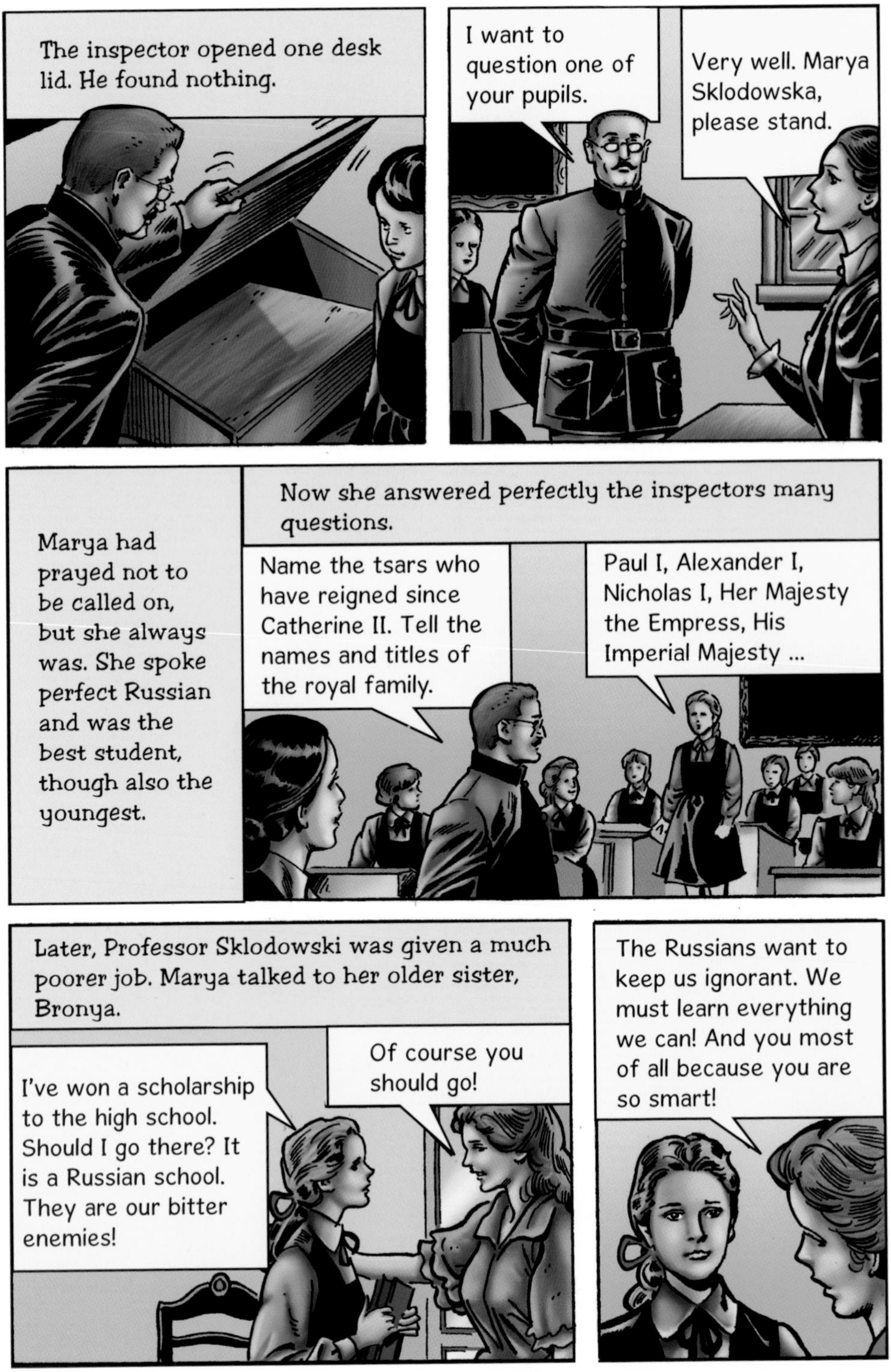

The inspector opened one desk lid. He found nothing.
I want to question one of your pupils.
Very well. Marya Sklodowska, please stand.
Marya had prayed not to be called on, but she always was. She spoke perfect Russian and was the best student, though also the youngest.
Now she answered perfectly the inspectors many questions.
Name the tsars who have reigned since Catherine II. Tell the names and titles of the royal family.
Paul I, Alexander I, Nicholas I, Her Majesty the Empress, His Imperial Majesty ...
Later, Professor Sklodowski was given a much poorer job. Marya talked to her older sister, Bronya.
I've won a scholarship to the high school. Should I go there? It is a Russian school. They are our bitter enemies!
Of course you should go!
The Russians want to keep us ignorant. We must learn everything we can! And you most of all because you are so smart!

So Marya went to the high school. And in June of 1883, there were graduation ceremonies.

The gold medal for the best student goes to Marya Sklodowska!

Her father was very proud.

We have many relatives in the country who want you to visit them. You must spend the next year enjoying yourself!

But papa, I expected to go to work!

You are only fifteen years old. You spent most of your life studying hard! Now you must have fun!

So Marya went visiting. Her aunts stuffed her with good food. Her uncles taught her to ride horseback. Her cousins took her to parties.

Look, tonight I danced through the soles of my shoes!

Wait until there is a kulig,* you will dance for two days and nights!

* kulig, an old Polish winter tradition sleigh ride party moving from house to house

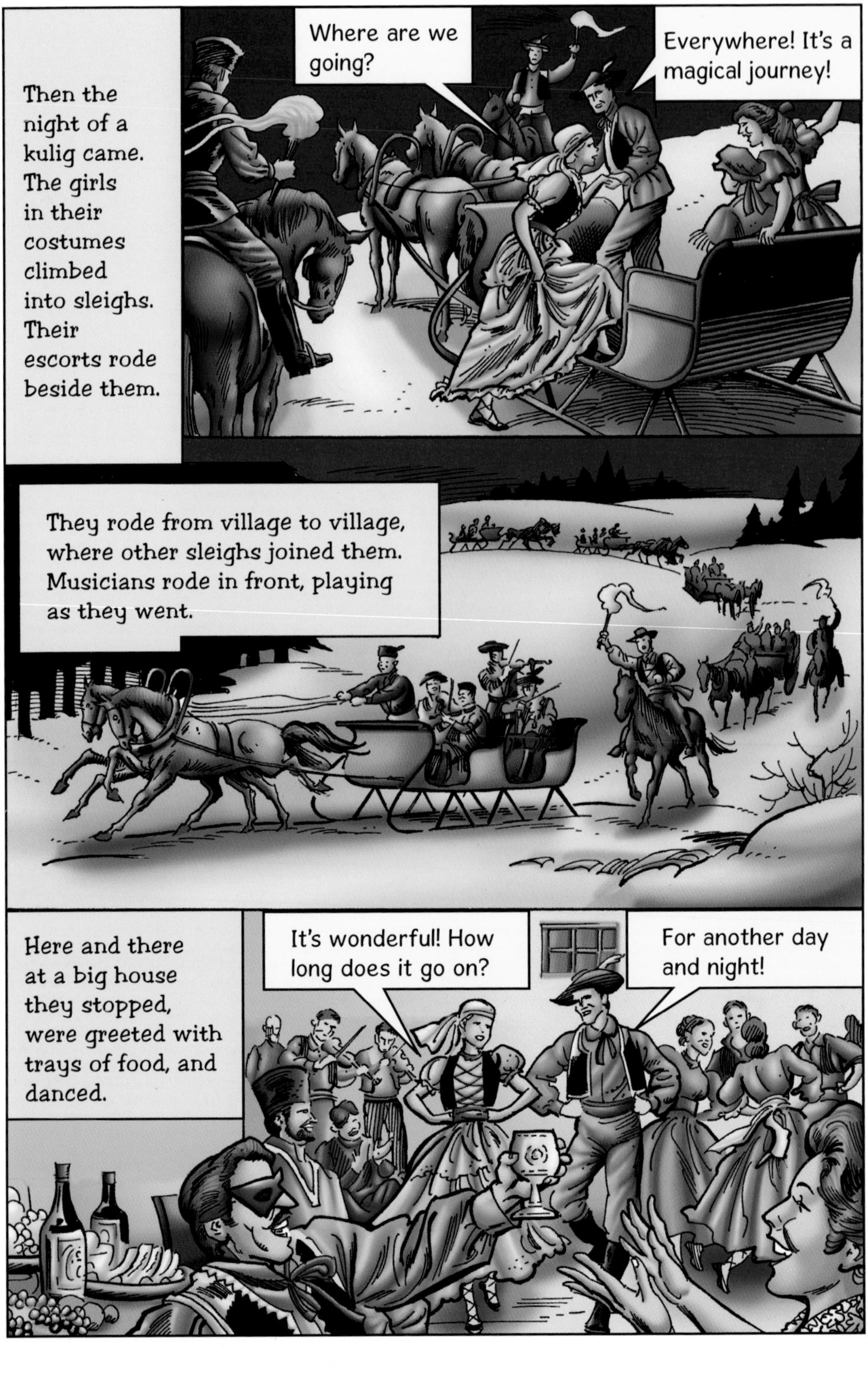
Then the night of a kulig came. The girls in their costumes climbed into sleighs. Their escorts rode beside them.
Where are we going?
Everywhere! It's a magical journey!
They rode from village to village, where other sleighs joined them. Musicians rode in front, playing as they went.
Here and there at a big house they stopped, were greeted with trays of food, and danced.
It's wonderful! How long does it go on?
For another day and night!

But the kulig ended at last. And so did Marya's wonderful holiday. In September she returned to Warsaw.

I want to earn my living helping you to study medicine.

You are a dear, but how will you earn this money?

I have written out these cards to send out: *Lessons in arithmetic, geometry, French, by young lady with diploma.*

But not many people wanted lessons. And those who did made it hard for Marya.

My son needs a tutor. You are much too young.

Sonny needs reading lessons, but he doesn't want them.

Yaaaa! I won't learn to read. So there!

I forgot to ask my husband for your money. I'll surely have it for you next week.

She seemed to spend her time tramping around Warsaw in bad weather. She made very little money.

I must take a job as a governess with a family in the country. Then the salary will be enough to help.

Live in the country? Leave papa? Why should you do that for me?

Oh, Bronya because you are older. You've been waiting for years! After you become a doctor, then you can help me!

So Bronya went to Paris to enter Sorbonne University. And in 1886 eighteen year-old Marya became a governess.

Miss Sklodowska.

Come in my dear! Take off your things! Warm yourself with hot tea!

Later she met the young family members.

This is Bronka, my oldest daughter. Andzia and Julek will be your special pupils.

I am so glad you have come!

The family was friendly. Marya got along well. Then the oldest son, Kazimierz, came home for the holidays.

I've never known a girl like you. You dance divinely. You're beautiful. You ride and row. And you have a brilliant brain!

Marya, I love you. Could you love me, marry me?

Yes, Kazimierz. I do love you!

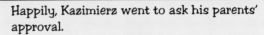
Happily, Kazimierz went to ask his parents' approval.

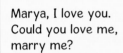

You, my son and heir, marry a governess? Never!

Oh, Kazimierz, you must be mad! You could marry the best catch in the neighborhood!

Kazimierz returned to school. Marya went on with her teaching. No more was said in the family of such a marriage.

I must stay here. Bronya needs the money I send her. I will forget love and go on with my studies.

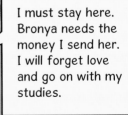

For three years, Marya worked with her pupils. In her spare time she studied. Whatever books she could find on physics, mathematics, and chemistry. When she had almost given up hope, things began to change for the better.

Papa writes that he has a better job. He can send money to Bronya. I should save for myself.

Spring came, and more good news.

Bronya has almost finished her studies. She is to be married to a young doctor. They want me to live with them and study at the Sorbonne!

It is too late for me. I am too stupid. Too many years have passed.

But at least she could return to Warsaw. She took a new job with a family there. She saw her father often. And in the evenings she visited a cousin.

The Museum of Industry and Agriculture! That sounds very important!

That is only to fool the Russians! The important thing is our small laboratory back here!

A laboratory where young Poles can learn science. You too, cousin Marya!

A laboratory, where I could learn to use the equipment.

From then on she knew what she wanted to do. She spent every spare moment in the laboratory. She saved every spare cent. At last she wrote Bronya that she could come to Paris.

For my passport, for my rail tickets, for my tuition. Oh, thank you, Father!

I can add this small bit, dear child.

The day came to leave.

I've sent my mattress, my bedclothes, my trunk. I have my folding chair for the train, my food, books, a quilt.

It won't be too long. Soon I'll come back to you and stay!

Yes, my dear! Work hard! Good luck!

12

Three days later she reached Paris and the apartment where Bronya lived with her new husband, Casimir Dluski.

At last, you are here!

Welcome, little sister!

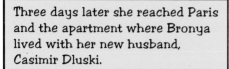

I will show you your room. It's small but quiet.

Please, could I first go look at the Sorbonne?

Following directions, she climbed to the open upper deck of a bus.

France! Where the air is free. The people are free. There are no Russian spies!

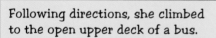

At last she reached her goal.

FRENCH REPUBLIC
FACULTY OF SCIEN
FIRST QUARTER

CLASSES WILL BEGIN AT THE SORBONNE ON NOV. 3 1891

The Sorbonne—where women are free to learn—where I am free to learn!

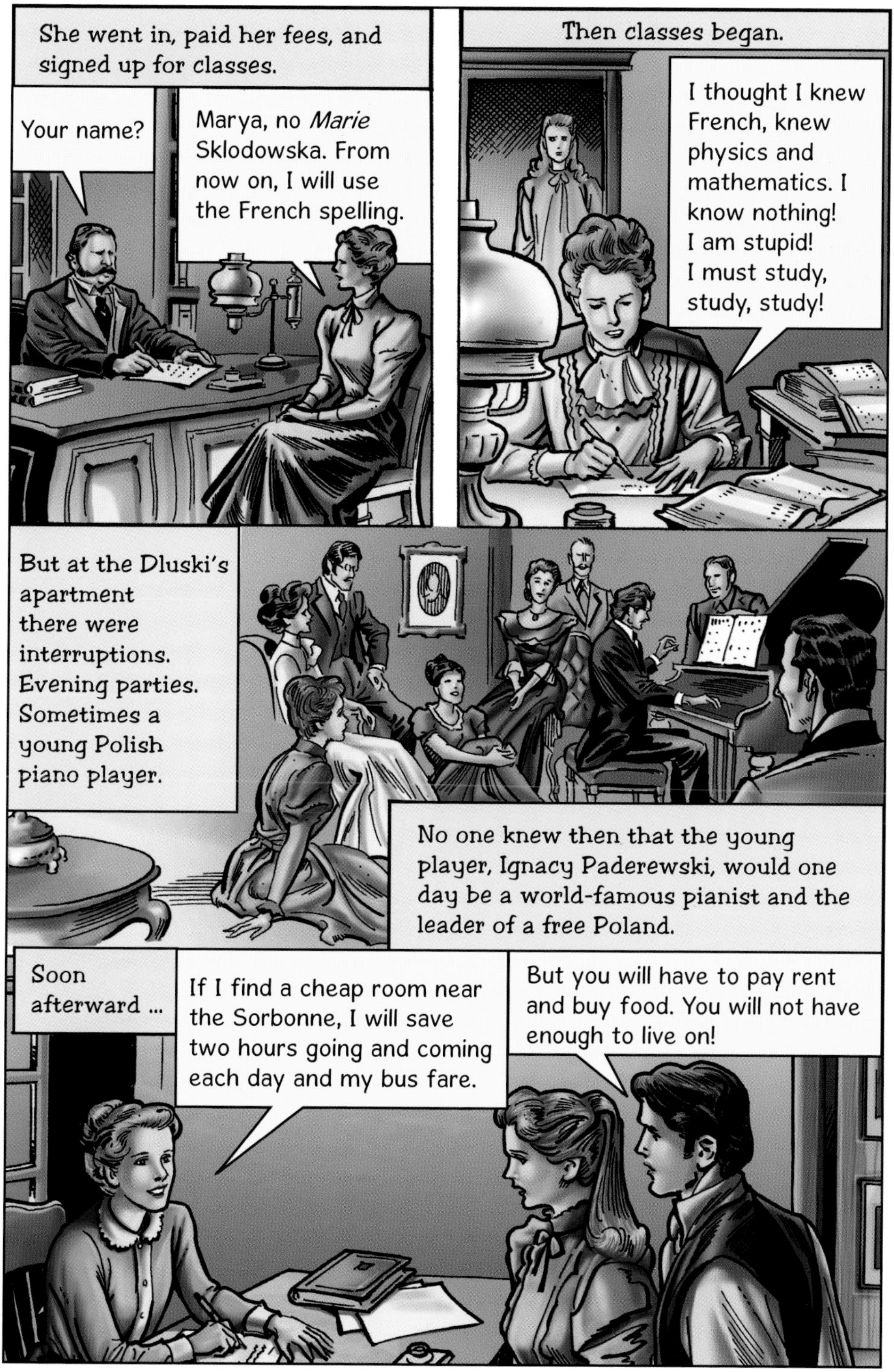
She went in, paid her fees, and signed up for classes.
Your name?
Marya, no *Marie* Sklodowska. From now on, I will use the French spelling.
Then classes began.
I thought I knew French, knew physics and mathematics. I know nothing! I am stupid! I must study, study, study!
But at the Dluski's apartment there were interruptions. Evening parties. Sometimes a young Polish piano player.
No one knew then that the young player, Ignacy Paderewski, would one day be a world-famous pianist and the leader of a free Poland.
Soon afterward ...
If I find a cheap room near the Sorbonne, I will save two hours going and coming each day and my bus fare.
But you will have to pay rent and buy food. You will not have enough to live on!

But Marie insisted. Soon she moved to an attic room with only a lamp for light, a small alcohol stove for heat, a pitcher to bring water from downstairs.

No one bothered her. She could study until 2 a.m. and start again at 6 a.m.!

She also forgot to eat. She grew pale and thin. One day she fainted on the stairs. A friend ran for Casimir Dluski.

Marya! What's wrong?

The little one has been starving herself. Put her to bed and feed her beefsteaks!

But no one could stop Marie from studying. And after final examinations, the results were announced.

First in order of merit, Mademoiselle Marie Sklodowska!

After a few summer months in Warsaw, she returned to Paris well-rested, fed, and with money from a scholarship.

Soon she spoke to friends about a problem.

I have a chance to do some research on my own. But I have no laboratory large enough for the equipment I need.

I will speak to a friend of mine, a fine scientist, who might have a workroom large enough that you could use.

Perhaps you know him, Pierre Curie.

Of course! He is a great scientist, head of the physics and chemistry laboratory—too brilliant to bother with my little experiments!

But she was persuaded to return the next day to meet him.

Pierre, I want you to meet Marie Sklodowska.

From then on, Pierre saw Marie as often as possible. He fell in love. Before she returned to Poland again, he asked her to marry him.

Oh, Pierre, long ago I decided to put science first and never marry!

And I decided the same! But I never expected to meet a girl who shared my ideals about science!

No, I must go home, take care of Papa, teach, do what I can for my country.

But in Poland, you can't go on with your studies. You must not give up your work.

Marie did leave Pierre and Paris to return to Warsaw and her father.

But she returned to Paris in the fall. And Pierre would not give up. At last Marie admitted that she loved him.

We can be married at my parents' home at Sceaux. They love you very much!

And I love them. They remind me of my own family.

They were married on July 26, 1895. They rode away on new bicycles for a trip through the countryside, as their relatives and friends waved goodbye.

She will be happy with my Pierre. There's no one on earth to equal him!

And you will have a loving daughter in Marie!

When they returned to Paris, Marie bought a cookbook and asked Bronya for help. She had starved herself, but she wanted to feed Pierre well.

Why do your dishes turn out so good, and mine turn out a mess?

You will learn! You've never kept house before.

In September 1897 a daughter was born. They named her Irene.

Is she not the most beautiful baby you've ever seen?

Absolutely the most beautiful!

But Marie still went to the laboratory for eight hours every day, leaving the baby with a nurse.

You will take her to the park for fresh air and sunshine?

Yes, indeed, Madame!

And she and Pierre spent their evenings studying.

We have talked of Becquerel's* discovery of the strange rays given off by uranium. I want to find out what causes those rays.

A fine idea! You may find something important!

I'll need a place to work and room to test many samples!

I'll speak to the school director. There must be a room there you can use!

* French physicist, Henri Becquerel, discovered that a mysterious X-ray was produced by uranium

She was offered a glassed-in porch, unheated and damp. She took it and went to work.

I know that the strength of radiation depends on the amount of uranium in the sample. And it is not affected by heat or light. Where does it come from? Is it present in any other metals?

She got samples of other chemical elements and began examining them.

Pierre! I found today that thorium gives off rays just like uranium!

You are a true scientist!

Do you think we might call this strange radiance radioactivity? And the elements that give off the rays are radioactive? Yes, I like it!

Then Marie did tests to learn the amount of radioactivity in her samples. The results surprised her.

I have done my tests over and over. There is no mistake. There is far more radioactivity here than the amount of uranium this sample could produce!

Of course, she talked it over with Pierre.

You see what it means, Pierre? If I have made no mistake, there must be an unknown element present causing this powerful radiation! A new element!

I know you, Marie! You've made no mistake. You have made an important discovery!

If so, could we call it polonium? In honor of my country?

Seeing the importance of Marie's work, Pierre put his own aside in order to help her. Soon their tests showed that there must be two unknown elements in the uranium-bearing ore.

And the second is much stronger, more radiant, than the first. Perhaps we should name it radium?

Find it, and you may call it anything you wish!

The Curies knew many things about what these new radioactive elements could do. But for other scientists to believe in them, they had to see them, weigh them, feel them.

Then we must find salts of pure radium to prove it!

If it is true, what you claim will upset beliefs scientists have held for hundreds of years.

It was in pitchblende* ore that Marie had found signs of the new elements. But in such small amounts that they would need tons of pitchblende to find the proof.

How can we afford it? And where will we find room to work with so much of it?

At the mines, they remove the uranium salts to use in glassware, then discard the rest. Perhaps we could buy the discarded ore for very little!

For a place to work—we have been offered this old shed.

A leaking room, no heat, no floor, but we will use it!

A friend arranged for the Curie's to receive the pitchblende dumpings by paying only transportation costs. At last it arrived!

Our pitchblende! It is here!

You are like a child with a birthday gift!

Then Marie became a one-woman factory, working in the courtyard more often than indoors.

I will find the new elements if I must treat a mountain of pitchblende!

* pitchblende, brown to black mineral that is the chief source of uranium

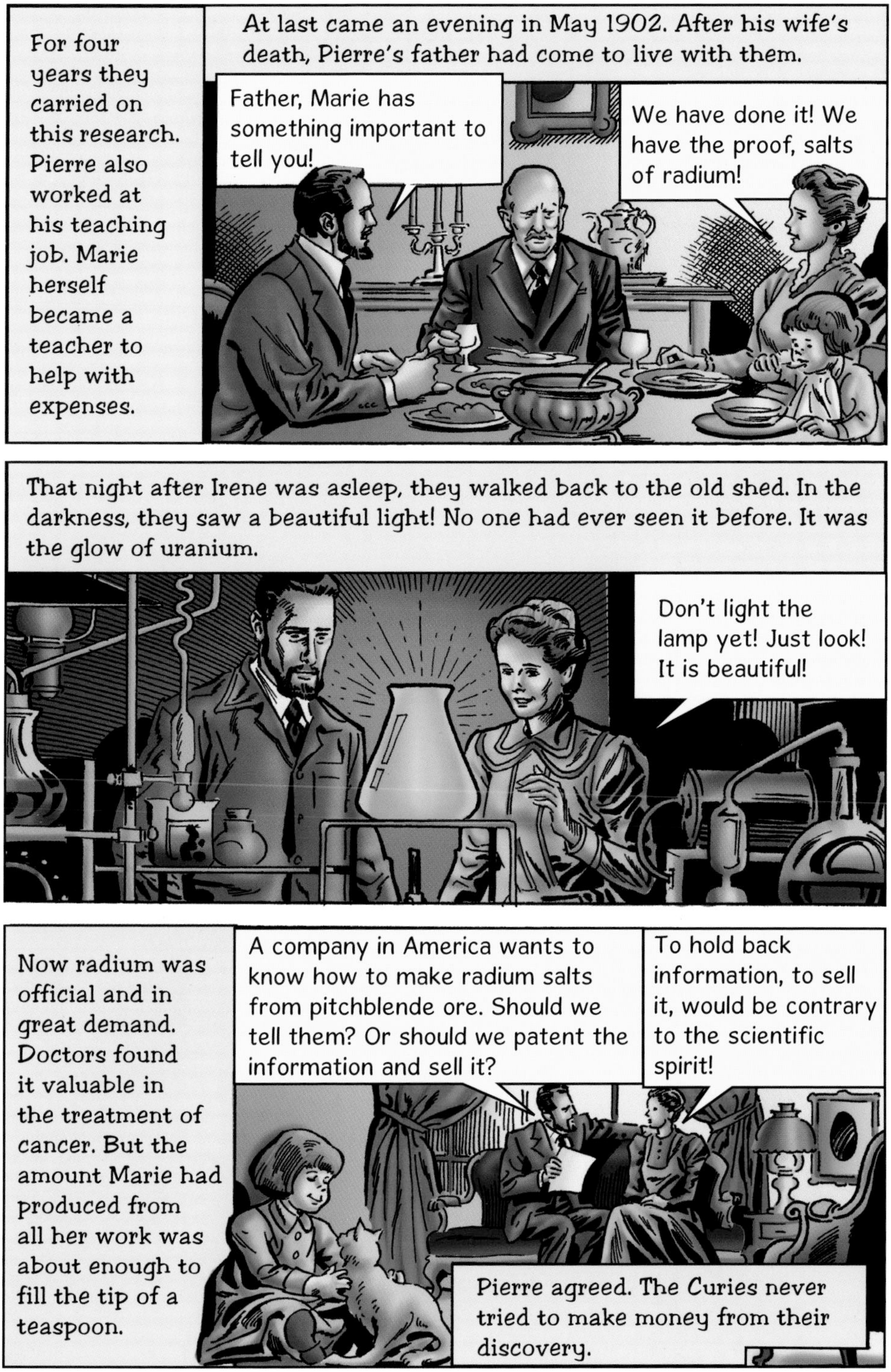
For four years they carried on this research. Pierre also worked at his teaching job. Marie herself became a teacher to help with expenses.
At last came an evening in May 1902. After his wife's death, Pierre's father had come to live with them.
Father, Marie has something important to tell you!
We have done it! We have the proof, salts of radium!
That night after Irene was asleep, they walked back to the old shed. In the darkness, they saw a beautiful light! No one had ever seen it before. It was the glow of uranium.
Don't light the lamp yet! Just look! It is beautiful!
Now radium was official and in great demand. Doctors found it valuable in the treatment of cancer. But the amount Marie had produced from all her work was about enough to fill the tip of a teaspoon.
A company in America wants to know how to make radium salts from pitchblende ore. Should we tell them? Or should we patent the information and sell it?
To hold back information, to sell it, would be contrary to the scientific spirit!
Pierre agreed. The Curies never tried to make money from their discovery.

In June 1903 for the work she had done, Marie won her Doctor of Science degree.

In the name of the jury, Madame, I wish to express to you all our congratulations!

The Royal Society of London invited Pierre to lecture, and gave them its Davy Medal.

You are the first woman ever to attend a Royal Society meeting—proof of your fame, Madame!

I don't think I like being famous. It takes too much time.

In December it was announced that the great Nobel Prize in Physics had been given to them and Henri Becquerel.

Oh, Pierre, 70,000 francs! Now you can give up the teaching that takes so much of your time!

And perhaps we can hire a lab assistant!

In 1904 Pierre was made Professor of Physics at the Sorbonne, and the Curies had a new daughter.

Is she not beautiful, your baby sister, Eve?

Yes, like a little doll.

In 1906 the Curies rented a cottage for the Easter holidays. It was a happy time.

Life has been very wonderful with you, Marie.

It rained the day after they came home. Marie came back later from a shopping trip. She found two old friends with Dr. Curie. Their faces frightened her.

Marie, there has been an accident. Pierre was crossing the street, a big horse-drawn truck was coming. He slipped. Marie, Pierre is dead.

Pierre is dead? Dead? Truly dead?

She walked past them into the wet garden.

I said to Pierre once that we could not exist without each other.

Pierre said, "You are wrong! Even if one has to go on like a body without a soul, one must work just the same!" I will try.

Soon she was offered the Physics professorship at the Sorbonne that Pierre had held.

You are the first woman ever to be offered such a job in France!

I will try to carry on Pierre's work, and to support our children.

On November 5, the Hall of Science was crowded with students, reporters, and the public. Madam Curie was to give her first lecture. She entered, made a stiff little bow, and began to speak.

When one considers the progress that has been made in physics in the past ten years ...

She had begun her lecture exactly at the point where Pierre had stopped in his own notes.

She won many honors and prizes including a second Nobel Prize in 1911. She was more concerned with the New Institute of Radium being built in Paris.

It is on Rue Pierre Curie. It will hold the wonderful new laboratory Pierre always dreamed of!

INSTITUT DE RADIUM

PAVILLON CURIE

RUE PIERRE CURIE

Marie herself would head the laboratory for many years.

In 1921 with Eve and Irene, she visited the United States. At the White House, President Harding presented her with a gram of radium paid for by donations from American women.

Irene and the young scientist she married, Frederic Joliot, continued the work of the Curies. In 1935 they would share a Nobel Prize for the discovery of artificial radioactivity.

They spoke well, didn't they? We're back in the fine days of the old laboratory!

Marie Curie died in 1934 of leukemia from the radium she had worked with for so many years. She laid the cornerstone on which scientists have built the Atomic Age.

Her last book was published a year later.

RADIOACTIVITY

RADIOACTIVITY

CURIE

MME. PIERRE CURIE
Professor
at the
SORBONNE
NOBEL PRIZE
IN
PHYSICS
NOBEL PRIZE
IN
CHEMISTRY

THE END